Outdoor Skills

Written by
**Mort Greenberg &
Carly Greenberg**

Forward

Within these pages lies a guidebook and a gateway to understanding our connection with the natural world.

As you stand at a crucial juncture, balancing between childhood wonder and the responsibilities of being a young adult getting outdoors is a special experience to take full advantage of.

This book aims to harness that energy and curiosity, equipping you with the skills you need to explore safely and responsibly.

Remember, the great outdoors is not just a place but a living, breathing entity. It has the power to challenge, inspire, and heal.

Our wish is that, with this guide in hand, you'll embark on your own adventures, forge your own memories, and nurture a lifelong respect for the environment and all its wonders. So, lace up your boots, pack your gear, and get outside. Adventure awaits.

Copyright © 2025 by
Mort Greenberg & Carly Greenberg

Design: Heri Susanto
Illustrations: Dian Kartika Abidin

First Paperback edition May 2025

ISBN: 978-1-961059-07-8

Published by TuckEmIn
www.tuckemin.com

Introduction

Tuck Em' In Publishing is a father-and-daughter effort that creates and publishes books for kids. Our mission is to Motivate and Inspire. Our vision is to help kids make the most of their todays and tomorrows.

The Fearless Girl and The Little Guy with Greatness is a book series that aims to share the following message: anything is possible for any kid if they put their mind to it.

Kids, you can find ways to handle yourselves in critical, real-life situations in our books. Caregivers, you will find ways to push the kids in your life to be their best selves. Through our books, we encourage families to communicate more effectively with each other.

"Outdoor Skills" is the 8th installment in The Fearless Girl and The Little Guy with Greatness book series. This book will move through 9 topics: 1) Basic Outdoor Principles, 2) Basic Survival Skills, 3) Situational Awareness, 4) Crisis Management, 5) Navigation and Movement, 6) Connecting with Nature, 7) Working as a Team, 8) Advanced Outdoor Knowledge, and 9) Ethical Hunting And Wilderness Sustenance.

Mort Greenberg and his daughter, **Carly Greenberg**, have embarked on numerous adventures together across the mountains of the United States. They also built self-guided, 18-hour day races in London, Paris, Milan, Venice, Murano, Burano, Rome, Buenos Aires, Tigre, Montevideo, Valparaiso, Santiago, Asuncion, and more.

This father and daughter team has worked through and overcome the same situations that you, as a parent, are experiencing now with a young daughter or son. Each skill in the book is inspired by actual travels over the years from when Carly was eleven to twenty.

You Can Follow Mort and Carly on social media:

@mortgreenberg

@greenbergcarly

@mortgreenberg

@carlygreenberg

This Book Belongs to

_____

Today's Date : _____

Table of Contents

Basic Outdoor Principles

This section introduces the foundational principles of outdoor ethics. It emphasizes the importance of respecting nature, understanding one's responsibilities, and adhering to courteous behavior on trails. A key highlight is the Leave No Trace (LNT) philosophy, which ensures minimal human impact on the environment.

Leave No Trace (LNT) Principle

Nature is an amazing playground. Still, like every playground, we should keep it clean and safe. The LNT principles teach us how to enjoy the outdoors while taking care of it.

Plan Ahead and Prepare

Before you go outside, think about where you're going, what you might need, and how to stay safe.

Be Considerate of Others

Share the outdoors. **Everyone should be able to enjoy it!**

Leave What You Find

If you see a pretty rock or flower, it's best to leave it so **others can enjoy** it too.

Dispose of Waste Properly

If you brought it, take it back with you. **No littering!**

Travel and Camp on Durable Surfaces

Stay on the path. This helps protect plants and prevents erosion.

Respect Wildlife

Animals are cool, but remember to **look from a distance.** They need their space just like we do.

Minimize Campfire Impact

Fires can be dangerous. **Only make** one if you need to, you know how to, and also have adult supervision.

Try It Activity

Have a picnic in your backyard or a local park. Make sure you follow all the LNT principles while you're out!

Ethics and Responsibility

Nature has its own rules. By being responsible, we make sure that nature stays beautiful and everyone can enjoy it.

Nature's Value

Nature isn't just trees and animals; it's a living thing that should be **treated with respect.**

Our Role

We're not just visitors; **we're caretakers.** Let's help keep nature safe and clean.

Teaching Others

Share what you learn with friends and family. **The more people know, the better**

Try It Activity

Write a nature pledge where you promise to take care of nature. Share it with your family friends and ask if they'll take the pledge too

Trail Etiquette

Just like in school or at home, there are manners for the trails. It's like saying "please" and "thank you," but in the wild!

Noise Levels

Nature is a quiet place. Let's keep our voices down and **let everyone enjoy** the peaceful sounds.

Stay on the Path

Trails are made to protect nature. By staying on them, we **avoid hurting plants or scaring animals.**

Right of Way

If you see others, like hikers or bikers, **be polite** and let them pass.

Try It Activity

Next time you go hiking or walking, count how many of these etiquette rules you can follow. Can you catch yourself and correct if you forget one?

Section 2
Basic Survival Skills

In this vital section, you as a young adventurer will discover the basic survival skills essential for any outdoor excursion. Topics run from emergency first aid techniques to sourcing food in the wilderness. Each chapter equips you with practical knowledge to handle unexpected situations, ensuring safety and sustainability.

Basic Wilderness First Aid

Ouch! Sometimes accidents happen, but don't worry. By knowing some first aid, you can help yourself and others.

1. Preparation

- **First Aid Kit:** Always have a **basic first aid kit** that includes items like antiseptic wipes, bandages, gauze, adhesive strips, tweezers, pain relievers, and any personal medications.

- **Knowledge:** Familiarize yourself with basic first aid techniques. Consider taking a **basic first aid course** through any Red Cross Training and Certification program, **https://www.redcross.org/**

2. Assessment

- **Scene Safety:** Before approaching anyone, **ensure the area is safe for you.** This may include checking for threats like wild animals, unstable terrain, or environmental hazards.

- **Check Responsiveness:** For an unconscious person, tap and shout to check for a response. For someone conscious, ask them what happened.

3. Basic Life Support

- **Airway:** Ensure the person's airway is open and unobstructed.

- **Breathing:** Check if they are breathing. If not, initiate CPR.

- **Circulation:** For severe bleeding, apply direct pressure to the wound with a clean cloth or bandage.

- **Knowledge:** It is highly recommended that you sign up and take a Wilderness First Responder course. Groups like NOLS (National Outdoor Leadership School) offer courses in many cities, **https://www. nols.edu/**

4. Exposure to Elements

Protect the injured person from the elements—this might mean moving them to shade if it's hot, or covering them with an emergency blanket if it's cold.

5. Wound Care

Clean wounds with clean water, and apply antiseptic. Dress wounds with bandages or clean cloth to keep out dirt and contaminants. If you sustain cuts or scratches while in the wilderness, **it's essential to clean them as soon as possible to prevent infection.**

Prevention is always better than cure. When venturing into the wilderness, it's a good idea to carry a basic first aid kit that includes antiseptic wipes, bandages, gauze, adhesive strips, and tweezers. It won't weigh much but can be invaluable in times of need.

6. Bone and Joint Injuries

- **Splinting:** If you suspect a fracture or severe sprain, immobilize the injured area using splints made from materials like sturdy branches, tent poles, or other straight and rigid items. Secure them with cloth, shoelaces, or strips of clothing.

- **R.I.C.E.:** For sprains, strains, and other minor musculoskeletal injuries, remember Rest, Ice (or cool), Compression, and Elevation.

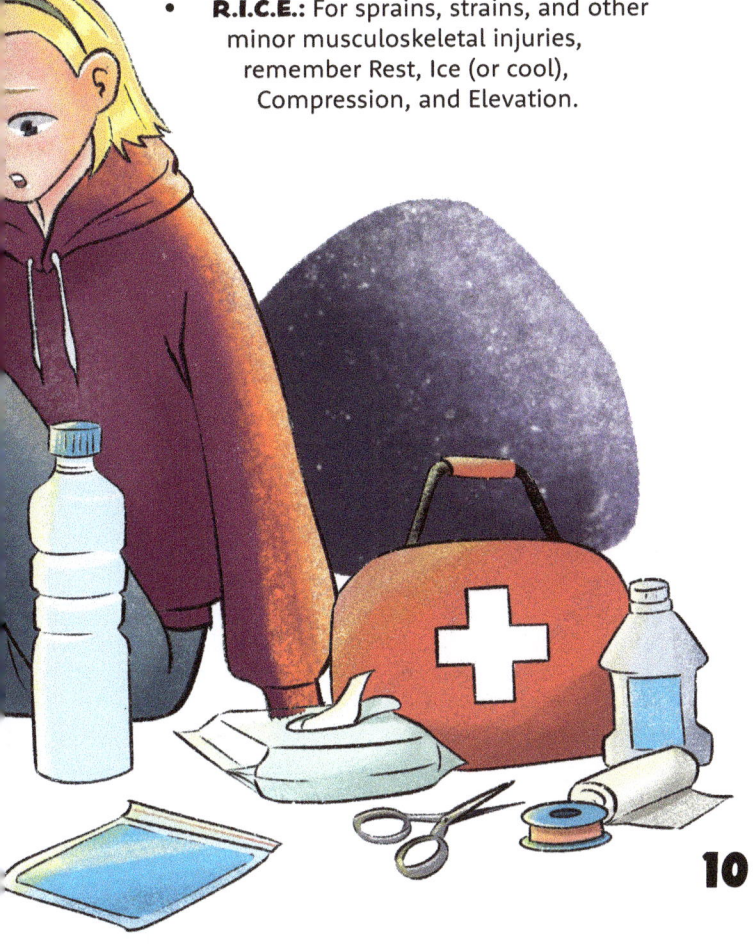

7. Recognize and Manage Hypothermia and Hyperthermia

- **Hypothermia:** If someone is shivering uncontrollably, confused, and showing signs of cold exposure, warm them slowly. Use dry clothing, warm fluids, and shelter.

- **Hyperthermia (Heat Illness):** Move the person to a cooler place, hydrate them, and cool them down with damp cloths or by fanning.

8. Hydration and Nutrition

Ensure the injured or ill person **gets enough water and food,** as the body requires energy and hydration to heal.

9. Evacuation Decision

Determine if you need to evacuate the person for professional medical treatment. **Factors to consider:** severity of injury, distance from help, weather conditions, and the injured person's condition.

10. Stay Calm and Think Clearly

A clear mind is essential for effective first aid. If you're unsure about what to do, stop and think. Remember, sometimes, **the best treatment is comfort and reassurance** as you wait for more advanced care.

General Guidelines to Help

Prioritize Safety

Before attending to the wound, ensure you're in **a safe location**. If you've fallen, make sure you're away from the edge of a cliff any other hazards.

Wash Your Hands

If you have clean water (like from a drinking bottle), rinse your hands first. If you have latex gloves or similar, wear them.

Clean the Wound

Gently rinse the wound with clean, cold water to remove any d or debris. **Avoid using stagnant water** that might be near you a can introduce more contaminants. **If you do need to use a stre nearby,** flowing water can be used if no other clean water sour is available. **If there are larger bits of debris** lodged in the wou that don't rinse away, use a clean cloth or tweezers (One of the most used tools you can have with you) to remove them gently **If you are using tweezers,** try to sterilize them first, perhaps by holding them over a flame for a few seconds (though rememb they'll be hot afterward).

Disinfect

If you have antiseptic wipes or solutions in a first aid kit, use them to disinfect the wound. If you don't have a commercial disinfectant, you can use alcohol (like from an adults flask or m bottle) to disinfect the area. It'll sting, but **it's essential to keep the wound clean**. While not ideal, in extreme situations where nothing else is available, you can use boiled water (cooled dow to clean the wound.

Dressing the Wound

If you have bandages or gauze, cover the wound to protect it fr dirt and further injury. If you don't have commercial dressings, use a clean cloth or even clothing that's as clean as possible. If available, use adhesive strips or tape to help close larger cuts. Blisters, don't pop them! Just **cover it with a bandage to preve further rubbing.**

Wound Care

Keep an Eye on the Wound

Over the following days, watch for signs of infection like increased redness, warmth, pus, or swelling. If these symptoms appear, or **if the wound isn't healing**, it's crucial to seek medical attention as soon as possible.

Stay Hydrated and Nourished

Your body needs resources to heal. **Drink enough water**, have electrolyte tabs or sea salt available, and eat nutritious foods if available.

Seek Medical Attention

Once you're back from the wilderness, it is a good idea to see a doctor, especially if the **wound is deep or if there's any sign of infection.**

Remember Tetanus

Cuts, especially from rusty or dirty objects, can expose you to tetanus. **Ensure your tetanus vaccination is up-to-date**, and if it's not, or you're unsure, seek medical advice upon returning from the wilderness.

Finally, while knowledge and preparation are crucial, nothing replaces professional training. Consider enrolling in a wilderness first aid course from a reputable organization before embarking on remote adventures.

Try It Activity

With a parent or guardian, create a small first-aid kit. Pack bandages, antiseptic wipes, and any other essentials. Make it a habit to take it on all your adventures.

Shelter Building

Knowing how to make a shelter can keep you safe and dry if you're ever lost or need to stay out in nature longer than expected.

Location

Find a spot **away from dangers** like falling branches or rising water.

Materials

Use branches, leaves, and other **natural materials around you.**

Stay Warm

Keep the shelter **small** to trap body heat.

Try It Activity

Have a backyard campout! Using blankets, branches, and other safe materials, try building your own shelter and spend an evening under it.

13

Water Purification

Water is life! But not all water is safe to drink. Let's learn how to make it clean.

Clear Water

Always choose the **clearest water you can find**. Avoid water that looks dirty.

Boiling

One of the best ways to purify water is **to boil it**. Ask an adult for help.

Portable Filters

There are **tools** that can make water safe. Always have one when you adventure.

Try It Activity

With adult supervision, try boiling water and letting it cool. Taste the difference between tap water, boiled water, and bottled water.

Fire Building and Safety

Fire can keep us warm and cook our food, but we must be careful.

Safety First

Always make a fire in a **clear area** away from trees or dry grass.

Starting a Fire

You need **tinder** (small, dry materials), **kindling** (small sticks), and larger wood.

Put It Out

Always **put out a fire completely** before leaving. Use water and dirt.

Try It Activity

Practice building a small fire with a parent or guardian in a safe area. Notice how the fire needs air, fuel, and heat to burn.

15

Knot Tying

Knots can be fun and super useful. There are hundreds that you can learn, but let's learn two basic, must-know knots you can use outdoors and indoors.

Bowline

A strong loop that doesn't slip.

1 **2** **3**

Square Knot

Great for joining any two ends of ropes

Try It Activity

Get a length of rope or a long shoelace. Practice tying each knot until you can do it without looking!

Food in the Wilderness

Sometimes, nature provides food, but we need to know what's safe to eat. Wild Plants: Some can be eaten, but others are dangerous. Never eat something if you're not sure. Fishing: It can be a food source, but always follow local rules. Food Storage: Keep food in tight containers t keep animals away. Here is more in-depth knowledge.

Safe-to-Eat Food Examples:

Dandelions
Every part of this plant is edible. The leaves, flowers, and roots can be consumed. The stem and latex can be eaten but are bitter and not for everyone.

Blackberries and Raspberries
Most people can identify these, and they're safe to eat.

Blueberries
Small, round, and blue, they grow on bushes.

Walnuts and Hickory Nuts
Found in wooded areas, but be sure you can identify them correctly.

Survival situations often demand resourcefulness, especially when it comes to finding food. While many plants and animals in the wilderness can serve as food sources, others can be toxic. It's crucial to remember that the best way to ensure your safety is to have prior knowledge and training in wild edibles from a reliable source, such as a local expert or field guidebook.

Wild Strawberries
Smaller than cultivated strawberries but have a similar appearance and taste.

Mulberries
These grow on trees and look somewhat like elongated raspberries.

Acorns
From oak trees, they can be bitter due to tannins but can be leached out by soaking in water.

Wild Animals
Are edible, but you need the skill to catch and prepare them. Examples include fish, birds, mammals like rabbits and deer, and some insects like crickets and grasshoppers.

General Rules

Plants to Avoid:

- ❌ Milky or discolored sap
- ❌ Beans, bulbs, or seeds inside pods
- ❌ Bitter or soapy taste
- ❌ Fine hairs or thorns
- ❌ An almond smell in the leaves and woody parts
- ❌ Any plant with umbrella-shaped flowers

❌ Avoid Mushrooms

Many edible mushrooms have toxic look-alikes, so it's best to avoid them unless you're an expert.

❌ Avoid Stagnant Water Creatures

Animals or plants from stagnant water might **carry parasites or diseases.**

19

Testing for Edibility:

You can use the Universal Edibility Test if you're unsure about a plant's edibility. Note that this test has its limitations, and it's better to avoid unknown plants if possible:

(!) Contact Test
Crush a small piece of the plant and rub it on your wrist or the inside of your elbow for 15 minutes. Check for any reaction like redness, burning, itching, or rash.

(!) Lip Test
If there's no reaction from the contact test, place the plant on your lips for 3 minutes, checking for any burning or itching sensation.

(!) Mouth Test
Place the plant in your mouth, but do not swallow. Hold it there for 15 minutes, checking for any adverse reaction.

(!) Swallow Test
If there's still no reaction, chew a small amount and swallow. Wait several hours. If you feel fine, the plant might be safe to eat. However, eat a small amount first and wait another 8 hours to see if there's any adverse reaction.

Remember, these guidelines are very general. In a survival situation, always prioritize known, safe sources of food. Before you forage in the wild, consider investing time in studying regional guides or taking a local foraging class.

Cook When in Doubt

Cooking can kill parasites and reduce the risk of diseases. However, **it won't detoxify poisonous plants.**

Try It Activity
Go for a nature walk with a parent or guardian. Look for wild edibles but remember not to pick or eat them without proper knowledge.

Section 3

Situational Awareness

Awareness is crucial in the wilderness. This section dives into tools, emergency preparedness, and understanding the risks inherent in various terrains and situations. It emphasizes hygiene, mountain safety, river safety, and more, providing comprehensive insights to navigate the outdoors confidently and securely.

Tool Safety

Tools can be our best friends in the wild, but only when used correctly. Safety is a skill that's as important as any other!

Knife Safety
Always **cut away** from your body. Keep the blade **sharp and clean.**

Axe & Saw
Use them with **both hands** and ensure there's space around you.

Store Properly
Keep tools in their sheath or case when not in use.

Try It Activity
Practice whittling a piece of softwood with a guardian's supervision with a safe knife. Always remember your safety tips!

Hygiene in the Outdoors

Staying clean isn't just about feeling fresh. It keeps you healthy in the wilderness.

Human Waste

Bury it **6-8 inches deep** and at least **200 feet from** water sources.

Litter

Pack out **everything** you pack in.

Clean Hands

Always **wash hands** or use hand sanitizer before eating.

Try It Activity

Practice the Leave No Trace principle on your next outdoor trip. Ensure you and your group leave the place cleaner than you found it.

Emergency Preparedness

Expect the best but prepare for the worst. Knowing what to do in emergencies can make a huge difference.

Stay Calm

Panicking can make things worse. **Take deep breaths.**

Emergency Kit

Always **carry essentials** like a whistle, flashlight, and first-aid supplies.

Signal for Help

Three short whistle blasts or shouts is a **universal signal** for help.

Try It Activity

Pack a small emergency kit with the help of an adult. Ensure it's light enough to carry easily but has all the essentials.

Mountain Safety

Mountains are majestic but can be tricky. Tread carefully and respect their might.

Weather Shifts

Mountain weather can change rapidly. **Be prepared** with layered clothing.

Stay on Path

Avoid shortcuts on trails to prevent erosion and risks.

Altitude Sickness

Ascend **slowly** and stay hydrated.

Try It Activity

Plan a short mountain hike with adults. Practice staying on the path and observing the weather throughout.

River and Stream Safety

Water can be deceptive. A calm river can have strong currents beneath.

Check Currents

Throw a stick to gauge the river's speed before crossing.

Try It Activity

During a day out, practice safe water crossings in shallow areas. Always ensure adult supervision.

Shoes On

When crossing, **keep shoes on** to protect feet and provide grip.

Cross Together

If with a group, **link arms and cross together** for stability.

Risk Assessment

Every adventure has risks, but you can avoid unnecessary danger with good judgment.

Stay Informed

Know the weather forecast and possible changes in conditions. And assume that weather can change very quickly. And, often what the local report may say can change at any time, so be prepared to adjust your plans as you see weather changing.

Check Surroundings:

Understand the environment. Are there loose rocks? Fast-flowing water?

Trust Your Gut

If something **feels wrong**, it probably is.

Try It Activity

Next time you're outdoors, play a game of 'Spot the Risk' with friends. Identify potential dangers and discuss how to avoid them.

Snow and Winter Survival

Snow is fun but can be challenging. Let's be snow-smart!

Dress in Layers

This **traps heat** and allows you to adjust to changing conditions.

Stay Visible

In snowy conditions, wear **bright colors** to be easily seen.

Avoid Hypothermia

Stay dry. Wetness increases the risk of getting cold quickly

Try It Activity

Have a winter day out! Play in the snow, build shelters, and practice staying warm. Always check for frostbite on fingers, nose, and toes.

Buddy System and Group Safety

The outdoors is more fun and safer with a buddy!

Never Alone
Always have at least **one person with you**, especially during challenging activities.

Check-ins
Regularly ensure everyone in the group is **present and okay.**

Decision Together
When in doubt, discuss with your group. **More minds can mean better decisions.**

Try It Activity
Plan a short adventure with friends. Assign a 'buddy' to each person and practice regular check-ins to ensure everyone's safety.

Section 4
Crisis Management

The wilderness can be unpredictable, necessitating both physical preparedness and mental fortitude. This section will teach you how to prepare for natural disasters, execute rescue techniques, and maintain emotional well-being during challenging situations. It underscores the importance of mental resilience in the face of adversity.

Natural Disaster Preparedness

Mother Nature is unpredictable. Knowing what to do during her fiercest moments can keep you safe.

Stay Informed

Know the **potential natural disasters** in your area — whether it's tornadoes, earthquakes, or floods.

Emergency Kit

Always have a kit ready with **water, non-perishable food, a flashlight,** and **a whistle.**

Shelter

Understand **where to take shelter.** For tornadoes, it's in a basement; for tsunamis, it's higher ground.

Try It Activity

With the help of an adult, assemble a disaster kit and make a family evacuation plan. Role-play different disaster scenarios at home to practice your preparedness.

Rescue Techniques and Evacuation

Sometimes, situations get tough, and we need to seek help or move to safety. Knowing how can save lives.

Signaling for Help

Three whistle blasts, mirror flashes, or large symbols (like SOS) on the ground can **signal distress**.

Stay Calm

Panic can cloud judgment. **Breathe deeply and think rationally.**

Safe Evacuation

Always move calmly and orderly. Running can cause chaos.

Try It Activity

With friends or family, simulate being lost. Use various signaling methods to get "rescued." Always ensure an adult is supervising.

CHAPTER 20

Mental and Emotional Well-being

The wilderness can challenge our minds as much as our bodies. It's vital to keep both strong and healthy.

Positive Thinking
A positive mindset can **overcome many challenges.** Believe in yourself and your abilities.

Talk
If you're scared or anxious, talk to someone. **Sharing can lighten the load.**

Take Breaks
If things get overwhelming, **pause.** Rest, breathe, and then continue.

Try It Activity
Start a wilderness journal. On your next outing, write down what you felt during challenging moments and how you overcame them. Reflect on these experiences and discuss them with trusted friends or family.

Adventuring in the wild is as much about mental strength as physical endurance. Every challenge faced and overcome adds to our resilience. Remember, with preparation, teamwork, and a calm mind; you can tackle almost any situation. Always ensure safety first, and never hesitate to seek guidance from experienced adults. Happy adventuring!

Section 5
Navigation and Movement

Navigating the vast outdoors requires a blend of traditional and modern skills. This section will give you knowledge on general navigation, star-guided night navigation, and the nuances of moving off-trail. With these skills, you as a young explorer can confidently find your way in the wilderness, day or night.

Navigation

Knowing where you are and where you're going is essential. Get the basics down and never feel lost again. In your own city, another city or out in the wilderness look at a map before you go out. Find the main features and know how to get around by looking at an online or printed map.

Understanding Topographical Maps

Topographical maps, also known as topo maps, are detailed representations of natural and man-made features of a specific land area. They show the shape and elevation of the terrain.

1. Map Scale:

- **What is it?** The map scale indicates the relationship between a certain distance on the map and the distance it represents in the real world.

- **How to read it?** For example, a scale of **1:25,000** means that 1 unit (like an inch or a centimeter) on the map is equal to 25,000 of those same units on the ground.

Try It Activity
Using a ruler, measure the distance between two points on a map and then calculate the real-world distance using the scale.

Maps

Learn to read topographical maps. Identify symbols, scales, and contours.

2. Legend/Symbols:

What is it? A legend is a key to the symbols, colors, and patterns used on the map.

Common Symbols:

- **Black Lines:** Usually represent man-made structures like buildings, roads, and railways.

- **Blue Lines:** Represent water features such as streams, lakes, and ponds.

- **Green Areas:** Represent vegetation like forests.

- **Red or Brown Lines:** Often used for contour lines, which we'll discuss next.

40

Try It Activity

Find a nearby landmark on your map (like a local school or park) and identify it using the map's legend.

3. Contour Lines:

What is it? Contour lines connect points of equal elevation. They give a sense of the shape and steepness of the terrain.

Contour Interval

This tells you the vertical distance (elevation change) between adjacent contour lines. For example, if the contour interval is 20 feet, each contour line is 20 feet above or below the one next to it.

Reading Contours:

- **Close Together Lines:** Represent steep terrain.

- **Far Apart Lines:** Indicate flatter terrain.

- **Closed Circles:** Often represent hilltops or depressions. If there are hatch marks on the inside, it's a depression.

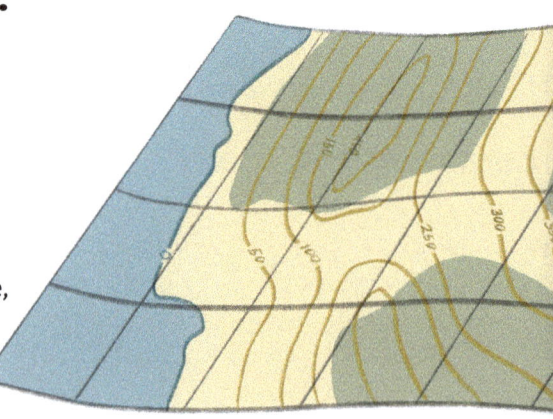

41

4. Grid References:

Many maps, especially topo maps, have a grid system overlaying them. These are often based on latitude and longitude or a coordinate system specific to the country.

How to use it?

To pinpoint a location, you'd read across the bottom or top for the easting value and then up the side for the northing value. The intersection of these values gives you a specific point on the map.

Try It Activity

Look for a large hill or valley on your map. Observe how the contour lines change as the elevation changes.

Try It Activity

Choose a random grid reference and try to locate it on your map. Once located, describe the terrain or landmarks in that grid.

5. Magnetic North vs. True North

Remember that most topo maps are oriented to magnetic north to help with compass navigation. However, some may also show true north, which is the Earth's geographic north pole. Be sure to align your compass accordingly.

Tips:

- **Practice:** The more you familiarize yourself with different maps and symbols, the better you'll get at reading them.
- **Combine Skills:** Use both your compass and map together for better navigation.
- **Stay Updated:** Landscapes can change, so make sure you're using a recent map, especially if you're heading into unfamiliar terrain.

Remember, a map is more than just a piece of paper; it's a gateway to understanding the world around you. The more you explore and use it, the more adventures you'll discover!

6. Using a Compass

Understand the basics of magnetic north, true north, and how to use a compass in conjunction with a map.

How to Use a Compass

Using a compass is a fundamental skill for navigating the outdoors, especially in areas where electronic devices might fail or run out of battery. **Here's a basic guide for kids aged 10 to 15:**

A. Understanding the Compass Parts:

Baseplate:
The flat, transparent bottom of the compass. It often has scales for mapping.

Orienting Arrow and Lines:
These are on the base of the compass and rotate with the bezel. They help align the compass with a map.

Compass Needle:
The red and white/black needle that moves freely. The red end always points towards magnetic north.

Rotating Bezel (or Azimuth Ring):
The ring around the compass face has degrees from 0 to 360 degrees.

Direction of Travel Arrow:
The arrow on the baseplate indicates the direction you should go when you've set your bearing.

43

B. Basic Steps to Use a Compass:

i. Finding North:

- Hold the compass flat in your palm at chest height.

- Ensure the direction of travel arrow is pointing straight ahead.

- Rotate your body until the red end of the compass needle (often called the north arrow) lines up with the orienting arrow on the compass.

- Where the direction of travel arrow points is true North.

ii. Setting a Bearing (direction to travel):

- Think of where you want to go in terms of a direction on the compass. For example, if you want to head East, that's 90 degrees.

- Turn the bezel until the desired degree marker aligns with the direction of travel arrow.

- Hold the compass flat and turn your body until the compass needle is inside the orienting arrow.

- The direction of travel arrow now points in the direction you want to go. Walk in that direction.

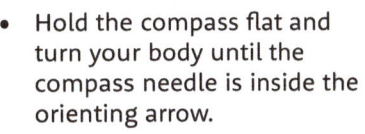

iii. Using a Compass with a Map:

- Lay the compass on the map so the edge of the baseplate creates a line between your current position and where you want to go.

- Without moving the compass, rotate the bezel until the orienting lines on the compass are parallel with the north-south grid lines on the map.

- The bearing (degree number) now at the direction of travel arrow is the direction you need to travel in the real world.

- Pick up the compass, and as before, turn until the compass needle is inside the orienting arrow. Follow the direction of travel arrow.

44

Astronomy and Night Navigation

The stars and night sky have guided explorers for centuries. Unravel the mysteries of the cosmos to find your way.

Constellations

Learn **basic constellations** like the Big Dipper and Orion, which can help determine directions.

North Star

The North Star (Polaris) gives a reliable **northern direction** in the Northern Hemisphere.

Moon Phases

Recognizing moon phases can help with **general nighttime** light expectations during outings.

Try It Activity

On a clear night, venture outdoors with a star chart. Identify at least five constellations and try to determine your cardinal directions using the stars. Remember, always have a buddy system in place.

Navigating Without a GPS or Compass

Sometimes, adventure takes you off the beaten path. Learn to travel through wild terrain safely and efficiently.

Terrain Assessment

Recognize what **types of terrains** (swampy, rocky, wooded) are easier or harder to navigate.

Safety First

Understand the **risks of traveling** off-trail, such as getting lost, facing wild animals, or getting injured.

Leave No Trace

When off-trail, **minimizing your impact's** even more crucial. Ensure you're not trampling delicate ecosystems or leaving any trash behind.

Try It Activity

Plan a day hike in a safe, local natural area with varied terrain. Try to move through different terrains, identifying challenges and discussing ways to navigate them. Always ensure adult supervision and inform someone of your whereabouts.

1. Celestial Navigation:

- **Sun:** The sun rises roughly in the east and sets roughly in the west, which can be used as a basic directional guide.

- **Moon:** If the moon rises before sunset, the illuminated side will face west; if it rises after midnight, the illuminated side will face east.

- **Stars:** The North Star (Polaris) in the Northern Hemisphere stays approximately in the northern sky. In the Southern Hemisphere, the Southern Cross can help indicate south. The Southern Cross is a group of five bright stars that form a cross shape in the night sky. Like those in Australia and New Zealand, people in the Southern Hemisphere can easily see it. It's important in their cultures and even shows up on some of their flags. The Southern Cross is also useful for finding your way. If you line up two of its stars and extend that line out, you'll find the South Celestial Pole, which helps you figure out which direction you're facing.

As a refresher, **the Earth is partitioned into two distinct hemispheres, the Northern and Southern hemispheres, separated by an invisible yet globally recognized line known as the Equator.** The Northern Hemisphere is home to the majority of the world's nations, housing approximately 90% of the global population. This hemisphere is characterized by a greater landmass compared to its southern counterpart. During the Northern Hemisphere's summer, the Southern Hemisphere experiences winter, and vice versa.

Try It Activities

1. **Sunrise and Sunset Directional Practice:** Wake up early enough to watch the sunrise. Stand facing the sun as it rises, and note that you are facing approximately east. Do the same at sunset to identify the west. **Materials Needed:** None

2. **Star Navigation Practice:** On a clear night, locate the North Star (Northern Hemisphere) or the Southern Cross (Southern Hemisphere). Walk in the direction it points for about 100 meters, then turn around and walk back. **Materials Needed:** Clear night sky

3. **Moon Direction Practice:** Observe the moon. Determine the direction you're facing based on the illumination of the moon, as described earlier. **Materials Needed:** None

2. Natural Indicators:

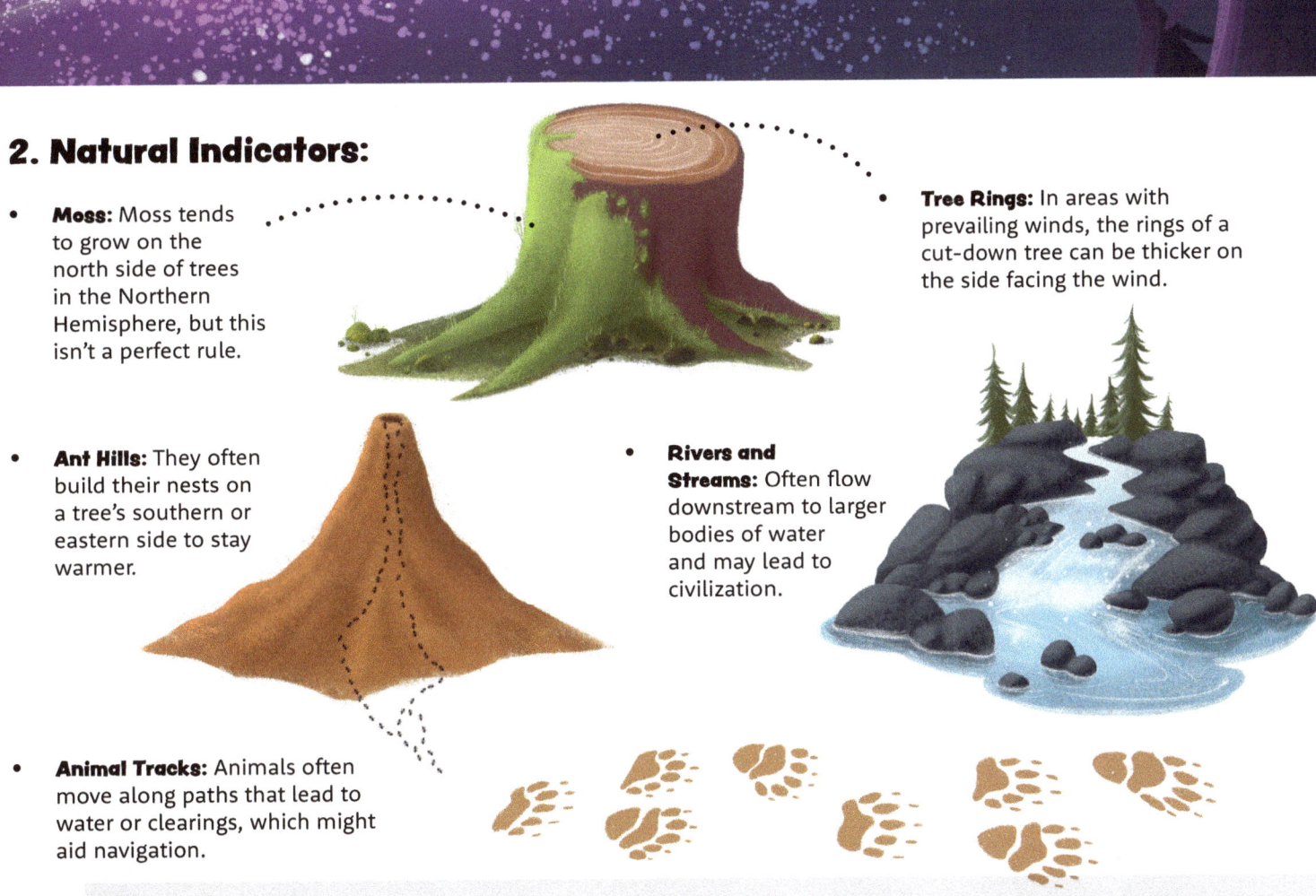

- **Moss:** Moss tends to grow on the north side of trees in the Northern Hemisphere, but this isn't a perfect rule.

- **Tree Rings:** In areas with prevailing winds, the rings of a cut-down tree can be thicker on the side facing the wind.

- **Ant Hills:** They often build their nests on a tree's southern or eastern side to stay warmer.

- **Rivers and Streams:** Often flow downstream to larger bodies of water and may lead to civilization.

- **Animal Tracks:** Animals often move along paths that lead to water or clearings, which might aid navigation.

Try It Activities

1. **Moss Direction Test:** Find several trees and observe which side the moss predominantly grows. Compare this with your known direction for validation. **Materials Needed:** Trees with moss.

2. **Tree Ring Wind Direction:** If permissible, and you come across a fallen tree, examine the tree rings to see which side the rings are thicker. **Materials Needed:** Fallen tree (**don't cut down a tree for this**).

3. **Ant Hill Orientation:** Locate an ant hill and observe which side it's built on in relation to a nearby tree or object. Confirm the direction with a compass if you have one for comparison. **Materials Needed:** Ant hill, optional compass.

3. Earth and Wind:

- **Wind Direction:** In various geographical regions, prevailing winds tend to follow specific patterns. These predominant wind currents can be categorized into three primary types: Trade Winds, Westerlies, and Polar Easterlies.

  - » **Trade Winds:** Typically found in equatorial regions, ranging from 0 to 30 degrees latitude, trade winds consistently blow from east to west. These reliable air currents are instrumental for maritime navigation and have been historically important for sea voyages.

  - » **Westerlies:** Occupying the mid-latitudes, specifically between 30 and 60 degrees latitude, the Westerlies are characterized by winds that flow from west to east. This pattern is consistent in both the Northern and Southern Hemispheres, significantly influencing these regions' climate and weather systems.

  - » **Polar Easterlies:** In the high-latitude zones, from 60 to 90 degrees latitude and nearest to the Earth's poles, the winds predominantly blow in an easterly direction, moving from east to west.

- **Sand Dunes:** In desert regions, the windward slope is usually gentler than the leeward slope, giving some directional indication based on prevailing winds.

Try It Activities

1. **Wind Direction Estimation:** Wet your finger and hold it up. Feel which side gets colder first; that's the side the wind is coming from. **Materials Needed:** None.

2. **Sand Dune Direction Test:** If you're in a desert, try to determine the prevailing wind direction based on the slope of sand dunes. **Materials Needed:** Desert landscape.

4. Sound and Smell:

- **Sound:** Listening for sounds of civilization, like cars or trains, can be useful.

- **Smell:** Sometimes, you can smell things that may give you clues about your location, such as the salty air near the ocean.

Try It Activities

1. **Sound Direction Game:** Blindfold yourself and listen for natural or man-made sounds. Point in the direction you think they are coming from. **Materials Needed:** Blindfold.

2. **Smell Direction Game:** Blindfold yourself again, and this time try to identify the direction of certain smells, such as food or a campfire. **Materials Needed:** Blindfold, various scents.

5. Man-Made Indicators:

- **Power Lines and Rail Tracks:** Following these can often lead to a road or populated area.

- **Signs and Markers:** Occasionally, you may find trail signs or other markers that can guide you.

Try It Activities

Follow the Line: If you find power lines or railroad tracks while hiking, follow them until you reach a landmark, then return. **Materials Needed:** None. But, only do this with an adult. Never go out on your own .

Methods for Maintaining Direction:

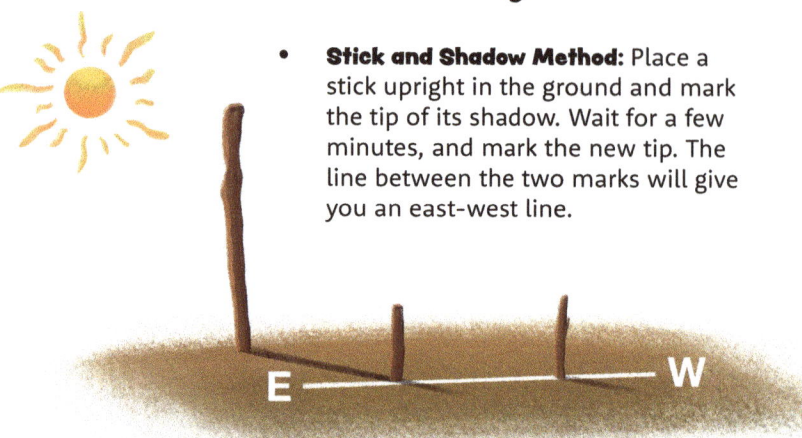

- **Stick and Shadow Method:** Place a stick upright in the ground and mark the tip of its shadow. Wait for a few minutes, and mark the new tip. The line between the two marks will give you an east-west line.

- **Watch Method:** If you have an analog watch, point the hour hand towards the sun. Halfway between the hour hand and 12 o'clock will be approximately south.

Try It Activities

1. **Stick and Shadow Method:** Plant a stick in the ground and mark the shadow tip at different intervals to find the east-west direction. **Materials Needed:** Stick, stones to mark shadow tip.

2. **Watch Method:** Use your analog watch to find direction as mentioned before. Validate your results using a compass. **Materials Needed:** Analog watch, optional compass.

Always Remember:

- **Leave markers or indicators:** If you're moving, make your path known for potential rescuers.

- **Stay put if lost:** Sometimes, it's best to stay in one place to make it easier for rescuers to find you unless you're sure about your direction.

Try It Activities

Marker Activity: As you walk in a certain direction, leave biodegradable markers, like stacking rocks, to mark your path. **Materials Needed:** Rocks or sticks.

Remember always to exercise caution and adhere to local laws and regulations when practicing these activities. Always validate your results with modern tools for the sake of safety.

Traveling in the great outdoors is both an art and a skill. With each outing, you'll become more proficient. Trust your training, always be aware of your surroundings, and remember, the journey is as important as the destination. Adventure awaits, but always ensure safety first! Before venturing into the wilderness, it's essential to plan, inform someone of your whereabouts, and take a map and compass, even if you use natural navigation methods.

Section 6
Connecting with Nature

A deep connection with nature enhances the outdoor experience. In this section, readers will learn about local wildlife, weather patterns, and the rich histories embedded within landscapes. Additionally, it introduces basic botany, conservation, and traditional indigenous knowledge, fostering respect and understanding for the environment.

Wildlife Awareness

Nature teems with life, big and small. Learn how to spot, appreciate, and stay safe around the wilderness's wonderful creatures.

Observation Skills

Spotting wildlife often requires a **keen eye** and quiet movements.

Safety Protocols

Learn how to act if you **encounter** a wild animal, be it a bear or a snake.

Local Fauna

Understand the **common wildlife** in your region.

Try It Activity

Visit a local park or nature reserve. Spot and jot down any wildlife you see. Later, research the animals and share your findings with your family.

Basic Botany and Plant Identification

Plants are essential to our ecosystems. Understand the green world around you.

Identifying Plants

Learn the basics of **differentiating plants** by their leaves, flowers, or bark.

Edible vs. Toxic

Recognize which plants are **safe** to touch or consume and which to **avoid**.

Ecological Roles

Understand how certain plants **contribute** to their ecosystem.

Try It Activity

During a nature walk, collect leaves from different trees (without harming them). Later, identify each leaf and create a

Weather Awareness

Mother Nature can be unpredictable. Equip yourself with the knowledge to face her changing moods.

Reading the Sky

Recognize signs of changing weather, such as cloud formations.

Safety First

Know what to do in case of **extreme weather events** like lightning storms or flash floods.

Preparation

Understand the **importance of dressing** appropriately and carrying gear for varying weather.

Try It Activity

Create a weather diary. For a week, note down the day's weather, then compare your observations with a local weather report. Discuss any differences with a mentor.

Traditional and Indigenous Survival Knowledge

Centuries of knowledge can guide our modern adventures. Understand and respect traditional ways.

Time-Tested Techniques

Learn **survival techniques** used by indigenous communities.

Respecting Traditions

Understand the **significance and sacredness** of certain methods.

Shared Knowledge

Recognize that this **knowledge is a gift** and should be used responsibly.

Try It Activity

Invite a local indigenous leader or elder for a chat about their community's traditional survival techniques. Listen, learn, and ask questions. Share your learnings in the form of a story or drawing.

Local Knowledge and History

Every place has a story. Discover the rich history and significance of the areas you explore.

Local Landmarks

Identify and understand landmarks' **historical or cultural** significance.

Respect for Sites

Learn the importance of **not disturbing or defacing** historically significant locations.

Traditional Stories

Discover **legends or tales** associated with particular sites or regions.

Try It Activity

Choose a local historical site or landmark. Visit it, learn its history, and present your findings in a short story or visual presentation.

Conservation Projects

The world we love needs our care. Get involved in projects that protect and preserve it.

Importance of Conservation

Understand why certain areas or species must **be protected**.

Get Involved

Learn about **local conservation** projects you can participate in.

Initiate Change

Even **small actions**, like litter clean-ups, can make a difference.

Try It Activity

Organize a small clean-up drive in your community. Collect trash, segregate it, and ensure proper disposal. Share the experience with peers to encourage more such initiatives.

Nature is a vast, interconnected web. Every bit of knowledge makes you a more informed and responsible adventurer. While these activities and lessons offer a start, there's always more to explore and understand. Remember to tread lightly, respect the land, and always be eager to learn. Happy exploring!

Section 7
Working as a Team

Exploring with others adds to the joy of outdoor adventures but also presents unique challenges. This section delves into the intricacies of teamwork, leadership, and conflict resolution. It's designed to empower young adventurers to work harmoniously within groups and navigate interpersonal dynamics with maturity and understanding.

Teamwork and Leadership

Adventuring is often a group endeavor, and every member plays a crucial role. Understand the value of teamwork and leadership to make the most of your wilderness experience.

Importance of Teamwork

Everyone has strengths and weaknesses. Learn how to **leverage the strengths** of each team member for

Leadership Qualities

Effective leaders **inspire, motivate, and guide** rather than dictate.

Shared Responsibilities

A good team shares tasks, celebrates achievements together, and supports each other during tough times.

Try It Activity

Team Obstacle Course: Set up a simple obstacle course in a park or backyard. Form teams and have each member perform a specific role (e.g., navigator, timekeeper). Discuss the experience afterward, focusing on communication and teamwork.

Group Dynamics and Conflict Resolution

Conflict is natural when different personalities converge, but how we handle these conflicts truly matters. Master the art of resolving disputes and ensuring harmonious group experiences.

Recognizing Conflict

Spot the **early signs** of tension or disagreements.

Effective Communication

Often, misunderstandings **can be avoided** by expressing feelings and thoughts clearly.

Problem-Solving Techniques

Develop strategies to address and resolve conflicts in a **positive manner**.

Try It Activity

Role-playing Exercise: Gather a group and assign each person a character trait (e.g., someone who's very stubborn and always wants to lead). Create a scenario where they have to make a decision together. After the role-play, discuss the challenges faced and ways to resolve them.

Building a team isn't just about finding people with the right skills but also about fostering a culture of respect, understanding, and open communication. From scaling heights to navigating treacherous paths, teamwork truly does make the dream work. Always remember: in the wilderness, we're stronger together.

Section 8
Advanced Outdoor Knowledge

For the more seasoned young adventurer, this section delves deeper into specialized knowledge and skills. Topics like clothing layering for various weather conditions, advanced signaling techniques, hiking best practices, and gourmet camp cooking ensure that you are well-prepared for advanced excursions. Here is to enjoying the wilderness to its fullest!

Clothing and Layering

Proper clothing can make a difference between a memorable adventure and a miserable experience. Dive deep into understanding the science and technique behind layering clothes in the wild.

Understanding Layering

The three main layers - base, insulation, and outer - each play a critical role in maintaining comfort.

Material Matters

Learn why materials like wool and synthetic fibers **outperform** cotton in the outdoors.

Adapting to Conditions

Adjust layers based on weather and activity levels to stay dry and comfortable.

Try It Activity

Layering Race: In a group, lay out sets of clothing representing the three layers. Race to correctly layer the clothing, discussing the purpose of each layer afterward.

Camp Cooking

Outdoor cooking can be a fun and rewarding experience. Understand the basics of nutrition in the wilderness and master the art of campfire cuisine.

Nutrition Needs

The importance of **balanced meals** during outdoor adventures.

Cooking Techniques

Using portable stoves, open fires, and understanding **fire safety** while cooking.

Food Handling and Hygiene

Proper storage, disposal, and cleanliness practices to **avoid illnesses.**

Try It Activity

Campfire Cook-off: Using a set of simple ingredients, come up with a meal plan and try cooking it outdoors. Discuss the nutritional value and taste-test each dish, and do this activity with an adult.

SOUP

Signal and Communication

In remote places, communication is vital for safety. Grasp essential signaling techniques and understand the devices that can be lifelines when needed.

Basic Signals

Using whistles, mirrors, and flashlights for signaling distress.

Modern Communication Tools

Gain an introduction and **research devices** like walkie-talkies, satellite phones, and personal locator beacons.

Ground-to-Air Signals

Techniques for alerting search planes or drones to your location.

- **SOS Signal Pattern:** Lay out three large rocks or logs in the shape of the letters "SOS". SOS is the international distress signal. It indicates an emergency and the need for immediate help.

- **Need Assistance:** Create a large "X" on the ground using branches, rocks, or any available material. "X" is the universal signal for "need assistance."

- **Need Medical Help:** Arrange rocks or logs to form a large "I" or the medical cross symbol (+). Indicates the need for medical assistance.

Try It Activity

Signal Relay: Create a "rescue scenario" where one group sends a signal, and another has to interpret it. Rotate roles and test out different signaling methods.

Hiking Techniques

Hiking is more than just walking outdoors. Learn about pacing, navigating terrains, and ensuring your backpack is your ally and not a burden.

Pacing and Stamina

Techniques to conserve energy on long hikes.

Backpack Fitting

How to adjust and pack a backpack for comfort and efficiency.

Navigating Challenges

Strategies for steep ascents, descents, and rocky paths.

Try It Activity

Backpack Balance Game: Fill a backpack with various items and adjust the straps. Have kids wear it and try simple balancing activities to feel the difference with a well-adjusted pack.

The outdoors is both challenging and forgiving. It rewards those who respect its rules and punishes those who take it lightly. Equip yourself with the right knowledge and skills, and nature will unveil its wonders. Remember, it's not about dominating nature but becoming one with it. Happy adventuring!

Ethical Hunting and Wilderness Sustenance

Hunting is as old as humanity itself. Before the rise of agriculture, our ancestors relied on hunting and gathering to procure food. When approached with respect and mindfulness, hunting can be a sustainable way to acquire meat and connect with the natural world. This section will guide young learners through the principles of ethical hunting, equipping you with the knowledge and skills needed to hunt responsibly and sustainably.

Understanding Hunting and Conservation

As we tread further into the world of outdoor skills, it's essential to understand hunting – not just as a means of obtaining food but as a practice deeply rooted in our history and the preservation of our ecosystems. Our journey through the ages of hunting will help you comprehend the bigger picture.

The History of Hunting and Its Importance in Human Evolution

Long before supermarkets and restaurants, humans relied on hunting to survive. It was a skill that provided food and materials for clothing, tools, and shelter.

Modern-day Hunting: Recreation vs. Sustenance

While many people still hunt for food, especially in remote areas, others see it as a recreational activity. Modern-day hunting is regulated by laws to ensure that it's sustainable and ethical.

- **Recreational Hunting:** Often done for sport, with specific seasons, and may or may not include consuming the game.

- **Sustenance Hunting:** Done primarily for food, often in areas where grocery stores are not easily accessible or in communities that value living off the land.

Try It Activity
Take a moment to think about the tools and technology we have today. Imagine going hunting with just a spear or a bow and arrow. Discuss with your friends or write a short story about a day in the life of an early human hunter.

Try It Activity
Research your state or region's hunting seasons and regulations. Why do you think these rules are in place? Create a poster or a presentation explaining your findings.

The Role of Hunting in Conservation and Ecological Balance

Believe it or not, responsible hunting plays a crucial role in conservation. By managing animal populations, we can ensure that ecosystems remain balanced.

For example, if deer populations grow too large, they might eat all available vegetation, causing problems for other species and the environment. Responsible hunting helps keep such populations in check.

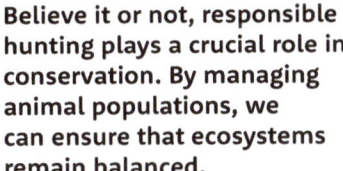

Try It Activity

Find a local wildlife conservation group or expert in your area and interview them about the role of hunting in conservation. You might be surprised by what you learn!

In Conclusion

As with everything we've learned, respect and understanding are crucial. When practiced responsibly and ethically, hunting can be a way to connect with our ancestral roots, obtain food, and even help our planet. Remember: Whether or not you ever decide to participate in hunting, understanding its history and role in conservation can help you make informed decisions and discussions about it.

Final Exercise

Write a short essay or draw a comic strip about a scenario where the overpopulation of a certain animal caused an imbalance in the ecosystem and how responsible hunting could provide a solution.

Note: Parents and guardians should ensure any practical exercises related to hunting are done in a safe and supervised environment.

37

Hunting Ethics and Responsibility

When stepping into the world of hunting, it's essential to know the techniques and have a deep respect and understanding of the life you're interacting with. Every experienced hunter will tell you that ethics and responsibility are at the heart of the practice.

The Principles of Fair Chase

"Fair chase" is a concept rooted in hunting ethics. It means pursuing animals in a manner that doesn't give the hunter an unfair advantage. For example, using technology that guarantees a kill every time or hunting animals in areas where they can't escape easily is against the principles of fair chase.

Respecting Animal Life and Preventing Suffering

Any life taken should be done with the utmost respect. Ensuring a clean and quick kill prevents unnecessary suffering for the animal. Also, showing gratitude and understanding of the sacrifice the animal made is essential.

Try It Activity

Discuss with friends or family members what "fair chase" means to them. Create a list of hunting methods you believe adhere to the principles of fair chase and those that don't.

Try It Activity

Watch a documentary or read a book about indigenous hunting practices. Take notes on how these communities respect and honor the animals they hunt.

Taking Only What You Can Use and Using All That You Take

Waste not, want not. This old adage holds particularly true in hunting. Responsible hunters only take what they can eat or use and ensure every part of the animal — from meat to hide — is utilized.

Try It Activity

Research how different cultures use every part of an animal after a hunt. Create a poster or a short presentation on your findings.

Understanding the Concept of "Trophy Hunting" and Its Controversies

Trophy hunting, where animals are hunted mainly for the purpose of obtaining a "trophy," like horns, tusks, or heads, is highly controversial. Critics argue it doesn't respect animal life and can harm conservation efforts, while some proponents say it can benefit local economies or fund conservation programs.

Discussion Points:

- Does trophy hunting support or undermine **conservation efforts**?

- How does trophy hunting **impact** local communities and economies?

- Are there **ethical ways** to engage in trophy hunting?

Try It Activity

Engage in a structured debate with classmates or friends about the pros and cons of trophy hunting. Use the discussion points above as a guide.

In Conclusion

Hunting is not just about the act of taking an animal's life. It's a complex interplay of respect, ethics, and understanding. As with all things, being informed and respectful will guide you in making ethical decisions.

Note: As always, parents and guardians should ensure any discussions or practical exercises related to hunting are approached with sensitivity and maturity.

82

Safety and Preparation

Venturing into the world of hunting isn't just about the hunt itself. True hunters recognize the immense responsibility they carry, not only for their safety but for others and the environment as well. Before embarking on any hunting adventure, it's crucial to understand and practice key safety and preparation measures.

Hunting Safety Rules: The hunt starts and ends with safety

1. Firearm Safety:

- Always treat every firearm as if it's loaded.
- Never point a firearm at anything you don't intend to shoot.
- Keep your finger off the trigger until you're ready to shoot.
- Ensure your target and what is beyond your target are clear before firing.

2. Arrow Safety (for bowhunters):

- Always keep arrows quivered until you're ready to shoot.
- Never "dry fire" a bow (releasing the bowstring without an arrow).
- Ensure you're using arrows appropriate for your bow type and strength.

Importance of Hunting Licenses and Understanding Local Regulations

Did you know that getting a hunting license often contributes directly to wildlife conservation? It's a system where hunters play a role in maintaining the balance of our ecosystems.

- **Why Licenses?** Obtaining a hunting license ensures that you are legally permitted to hunt and that you understand local hunting regulations and seasons. It helps manage wildlife populations and ensures that hunting remains sustainable.
- **Local Regulations:** Regulations vary by region, state, or country. These rules help preserve wildlife and their habitats. Always ensure you're familiar with local game species, hunting seasons, bag limits, and prohibited areas.

Try It Activity

With adult supervision, visit a local shooting range to learn hands-on about firearm or arrow safety. Engage with instructors to ask any questions you might have.

Try It Activity

Visit your local game and wildlife department's website or office. Gather materials on hunting regulations and licensing. Create a summary or a cheat sheet for your area.

The Role of Hunter Education Courses

You wouldn't drive without learning how to, right? The same goes for hunting.

- Hunter education courses provide knowledge on safety, hunting techniques, wildlife identification, and ethical practices.

- Most states require a hunter education course completion before issuing a hunting license, especially for young or first-time hunters.

Try It Activity

Research local hunter education courses. Write down the topics they cover, the duration of the course, and any other requirements. Discuss with a guardian or mentor about enrolling in one.

In Conclusion

Hunting isn't just a pastime; it's a privilege. By embracing safety, understanding regulations, and continuously educating ourselves, we can ensure that hunting remains a sustainable and honorable tradition for generations to come. Remember: The most successful hunters are always the most prepared and safest.

Note: Guardians and mentors should ensure discussions or exercises related to hunting are approached with care and maturity. Safety first!

CHAPTER 39

Basic Tools and Techniques

Hunting, one of the oldest traditions of mankind, has evolved over millennia. While the fundamental idea remains the same – to pursue and harvest game – the techniques and tools have seen great advancements. As young adventurers, getting acquainted with these tools and techniques is essential to ensure both efficiency and ethical practices during hunts.

Introduction to Various Hunting Methods

Each hunting method requires a distinct skill set, and understanding the basics will help you appreciate the complexities and challenges each one offers.

1. Bow Hunting

- **Traditional Bows vs Compound Bows:** Traditional bows, like longbows and recurves, are simpler in design. Compound bows use pulleys to assist with drawing the bow, making them more powerful.

- **The Challenge:** Bow hunting often requires getting closer to the game, mastering stealth, and having good aim.

2. Rifle Hunting

- **Basics:** Rifles use bullets propelled by gunpowder. They can be used for game big and small, but the type of rifle and ammunition should match the game you're after.

- **Safety First:** Always treat rifles as loaded, never point at anything you don't intend to shoot, and familiarize yourself with firearm safety rules.

3. Trapping:

- **What is it?** Unlike active hunting, trapping involves setting devices to capture animals.

- **Ethics:** Trapping can be controversial. Ensure traps are checked regularly and use humane methods to avoid unnecessary suffering.

Try It Activity

Discuss the pros and cons of each method with a hunting mentor. Which one do you feel most drawn to and why? Write down your thoughts.

Understanding Hunting Gear

Just like a painter needs brushes and paints, a hunter requires specific gear. This gear assists in making the hunt more effective and ethical.

1. Camouflage
Helps hunters blend into their environment, becoming less noticeable to wildlife.

4. Equipment Maintenance
Regularly check and maintain gear for longevity and safety. A well-kept bow or rifle ensures accuracy and safety.

2. Scents
Used to either attract game or mask human odor.

3. Calls
Devices or techniques that mimic animal noises to attract or communicate with wildlife.

Try It Activity
With the guidance of an adult, visit a local hunting store. Make a list of essential items you think a beginner would need. Ask store experts for their recommendations.

86

Techniques for Tracking and Observing Wildlife

Before you hunt, you must find. Tracking and observation are crucial skills for any hunter.

1. Signs to Look For

Tracks, droppings, feeding areas, and bedding areas can indicate the presence and direction of game.

2. Patience is Key

Often, you'll spend more time waiting and observing than actively pursuing.

3. Using Binoculars

For observing from a distance without disturbing wildlife. Learn to adjust and focus for clear views.

4. Respect Wildlife

Always maintain a respectful distance. The goal is to observe without causing stress or harm.

In Conclusion

Hunting is not just about the pursuit but also about understanding and respecting nature. You'll be better equipped for responsible and ethical hunting adventures by learning and honing these basic tools and techniques. Always remember: Knowledge, respect, and preparation are the hallmarks of a great hunter.

Note: As always, ensure any hunting-related activities or discussions are conducted under adult supervision and with utmost safety in mind.

Try It Activity

Take a nature walk in a nearby area, trying to identify animal tracks or signs. If possible, observe wildlife with binoculars. Document your findings in a journal.

Field Dressing and Processing

Harvesting game is only part of the hunting experience. Once the animal is taken, the next essential steps involve dressing and processing the game to ensure the meat is safe, delicious, and respectful to the animal you've taken. This chapter is all about understanding those crucial steps.

The Importance of Quick and Humane Field Dressing

When an animal is harvested, it's important to process it quickly. This not only ensures meat quality but also pays respect to the life taken.

- **Why it matters:** Quick field dressing prevents the growth of bacteria, keeping the meat fresh. It also makes the animal easier to transport.

- **Temperature matters:** Warm temperatures can spoil meat. Dressing and cooling the game quickly in hot weather is even more vital.

Try It Activity

Discuss with a mentor or parent about their experiences and the importance of quick field dressing. Take notes on their tips and tricks.

Basic Techniques to Process and Preserve Game Meat

Once you've field dressed the animal, the next step is processing.

1. Skinning

Carefully remove the skin, ensuring you don't puncture any internal organs.

2. Butchering

Separate the meat into different cuts. Depending on the animal, you'll have sections like steaks, roasts, and others.

3. Storing

If you're not cooking the meat immediately, you'll need to store it. This usually means freezing it in airtight packaging.

4. Safe Handling

Always use clean tools and workspaces. Wash hands frequently and ensure the meat is cooked to safe temperatures.

Try It Activity

Watch a demonstration on game processing, whether in-person or online. Document the steps involved and create a checklist for future use.

Utilizing as Much of the Animal as Possible

Out of respect for the animal and to minimize waste, hunters should strive to use as much of the harvested game as possible.

1. Bones

Can be used for broth or tools. Some even use them for crafting or decoration.

2. Hide

The animal's skin can be tanned and turned into leather products like clothing or bags.

3. Organs

Many organs, like the heart and liver, are edible and nutritious. They can be cooked in various ways and are often considered delicacies.

4. Other parts

Feathers can be used for crafting, and some even use antlers for various purposes.

Try It Activity

Research and list down various uses of different parts of an animal. Discuss with an elder or mentor how they utilize these parts in their hunting practice.

Note: Always ensure safety and cleanliness when working with raw meat. Always process under an experienced individual's guidance, and cook meat to the recommended safe temperatures.

In Conclusion

Field dressing and processing are essential aspects of hunting. They teach us responsibility, resourcefulness, and respect for the life we've taken. By mastering these skills, we ensure that we honor the animal to the fullest and partake in a tradition as old as humanity itself. Always remember: Every part of the animal has value. It's our responsibility as hunters to recognize and honor that value.

CHAPTER 41

The Role of Hunting in Modern Society

Hunting is a deeply-rooted tradition that has evolved with our modern society. Today, it's about survival, responsibility, conservation, and understanding broader impacts. Let's look at how hunting fits into our current world.

Hunting's Relationship with Modern Conservation Efforts

Conservation and hunting may seem like opposites to some, but they actually go hand in hand.

- **Population Control:** Overpopulation of certain species can harm the ecosystem. Responsible hunting helps balance those numbers.

- **Funding for Conservation:** Many conservation programs are funded through hunting licenses and fees.

- **Habitat Preservation:** Hunters often advocate for preserving wild areas, ensuring habitats remain for future generations.

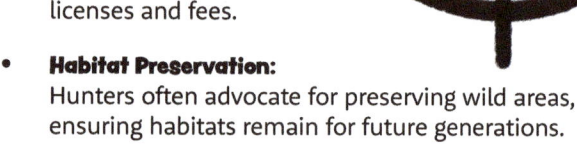

The Economic Impacts of Hunting

Beyond the environment, hunting also has significant economic implications.

- **Job Creation:** The hunting industry creates jobs, from gear production to guided hunting trips.

- **Boost to Local Economies:** Hunters buy gear, pay for lodging, and eat in local restaurants, supporting small communities.

- **Licensing and Fees:** The money from hunting licenses, tags, and stamps often goes back into wildlife management and conservation projects.

Try It Activity

Research a local conservation program funded by hunting. Write a brief report on its goals and achievements.

Try It Activity

Interview a local hunting gear shop owner or hunting guide. Ask them about the business side of hunting and its impact on the local economy. Summarize your findings in a journal entry.

Engaging in Conversations about Hunting: Understanding Different Perspectives

Hunting is a complex topic, and not everyone sees it in the same light. Here's how to navigate those discussions.

- **Empathy:** Understand that some people feel strongly against hunting due to ethical reasons or personal experiences.

- **Education:** Many criticisms come from misunderstandings. Politely sharing the conservation and economic benefits can enlighten others.

- **Active Listening:** Sometimes, listening more than speaking is essential. This helps build mutual respect.

Try It Activity

Engage in a mock conversation with a friend or family member, where they play a person against hunting. Practice addressing their concerns with empathy and facts. Reflect on the experience in a journal entry.

In Conclusion

Hunting in modern society is multifaceted, blending tradition with contemporary responsibilities. By understanding its role in conservation and its economic impacts and learning to discuss it respectfully, young hunters can be better prepared to navigate the complexities of this ancient practice in today's world.

Always remember: In all discussions, respect and understanding are paramount. Approach each conversation with an open heart and mind.

Hunting, when done ethically and responsibly, can be a way to connect deeply with the land and its creatures. By understanding its history, its ethics, and the skills required, young hunters can ensure they are stewards of the land, taking only what they need and giving back in the form of respect, understanding, and conservation efforts.

IN CLOSING...

Embrace the Great Outdoors! Our companions throughout this journey have been the call of the wild, the whispers of ancient trees, the silent tales of meandering rivers, and the starlit stories of the vast skies. If there's one thing to take away from this guide, it is that the outdoors is a treasure trove of experiences, knowledge, and life lessons waiting to be unearthed.

From the foundational ethics of respecting nature to the advanced skills that let you immerse deeper into the wilderness, every chapter was a step towards becoming a responsible and skilled outdoor enthusiast. But remember, knowledge is only powerful when combined with experience. It's crucial not just to read but to go out and practice, learn, and grow from real encounters with nature.

Moreover, always remember that the wilderness doesn't differentiate. It is impartial, and its vastness and unpredictability are what make it enchanting. Your respect for it, your preparedness, and your humility are your best tools. While this book equips you with knowledge, your experiences will mold your wisdom.

And while nature teaches us many things – survival, resilience, and wonder, it also teaches us about our own insignificance in the grand tapestry of life. This realization is not meant to belittle but to inspire a deeper respect for every living being and our delicate balance.

To every young adventurer reading this: your journey has just begun. Let the horizons call you, the mountains challenge you, and the serene nights under the stars fill your heart with dreams. Go forth with an open heart, a curious mind, and a spirit filled with respect for the world around you.

About The Authors

For the past 25 years **Mort Greenberg** has been a salesperson and sales manager for technology start-ups and larger media companies. Fighting his way up from an Account Executive to a role as a division President you can guess there were many challenges that needed to be overcome. Along the way Mort launched two companies, FitAd and MindFlight and learned many hard-fought lessons that start-ups are not always successful. He is a graduate of the State University of New York at New Paltz where he studied International Relations and Economics. While in college he started a company selling screen printing and promotional items to local businesses and on-campus organizations. At the same time, he also volunteered as a Congressional District Intern for the U.S. House of Representatives. He is an Eagle Scout and in junior high school bought several newspaper routes from neighborhood kids to create his first business. Mort is also the author of Revenue Vs. Sales, a three book series that you can find on Amazon.com.

Carly Greenberg attends the University of Maryland's Smith School of Business with a double major in marketing and mana—gement. Carly's twin brother has autism, and she has helped him find his voice through her unique interactions with him. He is the original little guy with greatness. Carly is the original fearless girl, always helping others, volunteering, and finding ways to do more with less - all while having to put up with a crazy dad. Carly also holds a black belt in Tae Kwon Do.